GW01157515

MICHAEL HURD

Adam-in-Eden

A CANTATA IN POPULAR STYLE
FOR UNISON VOICES (WITH DIVISIONS)
AND PIANO
WITH GUITAR CHORD SYMBOLS

NOVELLO PUBLISHING LIMITED
8/9 Frith Street, London W1V 5TZ

Order No: NOV 20019402

Cover by Dennis Reader

© Copyright 1982 Novello & Company Limited

No part of this publication may be copied or reproduced in any form or by any
means without the prior permission of Novello & Company Limited.

Permission to perform this work in public must be obtained from The
Performing Right Society Limited, 29/33 Berners Street, London W1P 4AA or
from the affiliated Society overseas.

Commissioned by the Thanet Schools Music Association and first performed at the Primary Schools' Festival on 24 March 1981 at the Winter Gardens, Margate, Conductor Robert Weaver.

DURATION ABOUT 21 MINUTES

NOTES ON PERFORMANCE

Anyone wishing to present this cantata in a dramatic, or semi-staged way may find it sensible to allocate certain numbers, or sections thereof, to soloists (with the chorus joining in, perhaps, at convenient moments). Exactly how this is done, and to what degree, must depend on local circumstances, but as a method of presentation it has my blessing. Similarly, the judicious use of drum kit and double bass is to be encouraged.

Michael Hurd

ADAM - IN - EDEN

MICHAEL HURD

© Novello & Company Limited 1982

All rights Reserved

new. / do.
Ev'-ry-thing is Pa-ra-dise in the gar - den.
I have made you lord o-ver ev'-ry crea - ture.

Ev'-ry-thing is gen-tle and good and true. So live, A-dam, I give, A-dam, My
Be their friend and ten-der to each his due. So grow, A-dam, And know, A-dam, My

NARRATOR. And so Adam entered

whole crea-tion to you.
trust is giv-en to you.

molto rall.   a tempo

into the Garden of Eden and, for a while, he was happy.
But as he looked around, he began to notice something rather odd . . .

rall.

segue

4

* Probably *Haemaphysalis bispinosum*.

I be the on-ly one, Quite such a lone-ly one? Why should I be quite be-yond the

I be the on-ly one, Quite such a lone-ly one? Why should I be quite be-yond the

pale!

pale!

NARRATOR. And when He heard this, God looked down from heaven and said:

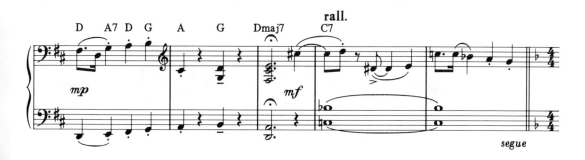

segue

wife for you. Set-tle down an' go to sleep, An', just for in-for-ma-tion,

While you're bus-y coun-tin' sheep I'll car-ry out an o-pe-ra-tion. A-dam, do as

you are bid. All I need to take a-way is one spare rib,— An', in the morn-in'

when you rise— I doubt if you'll be-lieve your eyes.

NARRATOR. And sure enough, when he awoke next morning, Adam was sore amazed:

segue

12

there was only one thing to remember:

Touch an - y ap - ples an' I guar-an - tee___ You'll re - - gret it in the
Touch not the ap- ples on the ap- ple tree. You must do as you are

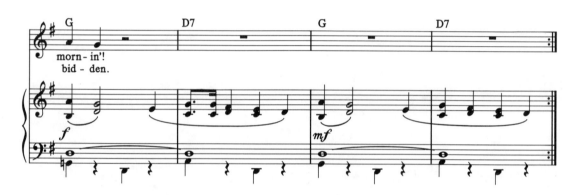

morn- in'!
bid - den.

NARRATOR. Adam and Eve did as

the Lord commanded. But as time went on they began to get a little restless.

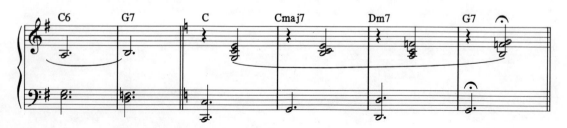

16

18

NARRATOR. Scarcely had they eaten the apple, than Adam and Eve began to feel very strange indeed!

NARRATOR. Then God, more in sorrow than in anger, pointed to the Gates of Paradise and said:

24

home. May-be you are not be - yond re-demp-tion. May-be through my love you will a -

tone? Though we part, A-dam, Take heart, A-dam, For mer - cy may be

shown. You'll nev - - er walk a - - lone.

poco rall.   a tempo

NARRATOR.* And that is ex - act-ly   how the world began.

* speak in the rhythm indicated.

3/99(33573)
Printed in England